The Poetry of James Shirley

James Shirley was born in London in September 1596.

His education was through a collection of England's finest establishments: Merchant Taylors' School, London, St John's College, Oxford, and St Catharine's College, Cambridge, where he took his B.A. degree in approximately 1618.

He first published in 1618, a poem entitled Echo, or the Unfortunate Lovers.

As with many artists of this period full details of his life and career are not recorded. Sources say that after graduating he became "a minister of God's word in or near St Albans." A conversion to the Catholic faith enabled him to become master of St Albans School from 1623–25.

He wrote his first play, Love Tricks, or the School of Complement, which was licensed on February 10th, 1625. From the given date it would seem he wrote this whilst at St Albans but, after its production, he moved to London and to live in Gray's Inn.

For the next two decades, he would write prolifically and with great quality, across a spectrum of thirty plays; through tragedies and comedies to tragicomedies as well as several books of poetry. Unfortunately, his talents were left to wither when Parliament passed the Puritan edict in 1642, forbidding all stage plays and closing the theatres.

Most of his early plays were performed by Queen Henrietta's Men, the acting company for which Shirley was engaged as house dramatist.

Shirley's sympathies lay with the King in battles with Parliament and he received marks of special favor from the Queen.

He made a bitter attack on William Prynne, who had attacked the stage in Histriomastix, and, when in 1634 a special masque was presented at Whitehall by the gentlemen of the Inns of Court as a practical reply to Prynne, Shirley wrote the text—The Triumph of Peace.

Shirley spent the years 1636 to 1640 in Ireland, under the patronage of the Earl of Kildare. Several of his plays were produced by his friend John Ogilby in Dublin in the first ever constructed Irish theatre; The Werburgh Street Theatre. During his years in Dublin he wrote The Doubtful Heir, The Royal Master, The Constant Maid, and St. Patrick for Ireland.

In his absence from London, Queen Henrietta's Men sold off a dozen of his plays to the stationers, who naturally, enough published them. When Shirley returned to London in 1640, he finished with the Queen Henrietta's company and his final plays in London were acted by the King's Men.

On the outbreak of the English Civil War Shirley served with the Earl of Newcastle. However when the King's fortunes began to decline he returned to London. There his friend Thomas Stanley gave him help and thereafter Shirley supported himself in the main by teaching and publishing some educational works under the Commonwealth. In addition to these he published during the period of dramatic eclipse four small volumes of poems and plays, in 1646, 1653, 1655, and 1659.

It is said that he was "a drudge" for John Ogilby in his translations of Homer's Iliad and the Odyssey, and survived into the reign of Charles II, but, though some of his comedies were revived, his days as a playwright were over.

His death, at age seventy, along with that of his wife, in 1666, is described as one of fright and exposure due to the Great Fire of London which had raged through parts of London from September 2nd to the 5th.

He was buried at St Giles in the Fields, in London, on October 29th, 1666.

Index of Contents

Dedication

To the Truly Noble, Bernard Hide, Esquire

Sir,

It will be a long Ambition satisfied, if by this, I have the happinesse of making my self more known to you, though in the same Act I put my self to a blush, that I have not a better present to excuse the confidence. If I do look upon you but as you relate to me in the common Interest and Fame of your vertues, wherein I share with others, I may be censured a bold man, since as they are proportioned to me, they are more then equall to the whole deserts of some that write both honour and abilities. But when I consider that graceful part of your Character, Sweetnes, which gives both the Price and Beauty to your other furnitures of Art and Nature, I cannot think my self without capacity of pardon for this application, the well meant tender of my service.

They are Papers in themselves not worth your eye, or to be numbred with those reserves of wit and learning that wait upon your recreations; and if they receive entertainment abroad, I shall acknowledge it rather a debt which men pay to your Name, then a merit of the Poems; and if they meet with the frowning world, I have subscribed my owne, to be accused for them, and this presumption. Howsoever, if they may enjoy but your smile and shade, which was the first choise of my thoughts, it shall incourage me to reach your worth with more sutable imaginations; till when, give me leave to write my self

Your faithfull Honourer,
JAMES SHIRLEY.

Poems in Praise of James Shirley

To My Worthy Friend Mr. James Shirley, Upon His Poems by Thomas Stanley

When dearest Friend, thy verse doth re-inspire
Loves pale decaying Torch with brighter fire,
Whilst everywhere thou dost dilate thy flame,
And to the world spread thy Odelias name,
The justice of all Ages must remit
To Her the Prize of Beauty, Thee of Wit.
Then like some skilful Artist, that to wonder
Framing a peece, displeas'd, takes it asunder,
Thou Beauty dost depose, Her Charmes deny,
And all the mystick chains of Love untie;
Thus thy diviner Muse a power 'bove Fate
May boast, that can both make, and uncreate.
Next thou call'st back to life that Love-sick Boy,
To the kind-hearted Nymphes lesse fair then coy,
Who, by reflex beams burnt with vain desire,
Did Phenix-like, in his owne flames expire:
But should he view his shadow drawn by thee,
He with himself once more in love would be:
Eccho (who though she words pursue, her hast
Can onely overtake and stop the last)
Shall her first speech and humane veil obtaine
To sing thy softer numbers o're again.
Thus into dying Poetry, thy Muse

Doth full perfection and new life infuse,
Each line deserves a Laurel, and thy praise
Askes not a Garland, but a Grove of Bayes:
Nor can ours raise thy lasting Trophies higher,
Who only reach at merit, to admire.
But I must chide thee Friend, how canst thou be
A Patron, yet a Foe to Poetrie?
For while thou dost this Age to Verse restore,
Thou dost deprive the next of owning more;
And hast so far even future aymes surpast,
That none dare write; Thus being first and last,
All, their abortive Muses will suppresse,
And Poetry by this increase grow lesse.

To My Honoured Friend M. James Shirley, Upon the Printing of His Elegant Poems by Thomas May

Although thou want the Theaters applause,
Which now is fitly silenc'd by the Lawes,
Since these sad times that Civil swords did rage,
And make three Kingdoms the lamented stage
Of real Tragedies, it was not fit
We quite should lose such monuments of wit
As flowd from thy terse pen: the Presse alone
Can vindicate from dark oblivion
Thy Poems, Friend; those that with skill can read,
Shall be thy Judges now, and shall instead
Of ignorant spectators, grace thy name,
Though with a narrower, yet a truer Fame,
And crown with longer life thy worthy pains.
All Muses are not guiltlesse; but such strains
As thine, deserve, if I may verdict give,
In sober, chast, and learned times to live.

To His Honoured Friend, the Author, Upon His Poems by George Bucke

Whilst I am in thy Poem, I am lead
Through a rich Gallery, in which are spread
The choicest Pictures of true skill and height,
Where every pause is Rapture and Delight.
Here, by thy Fancy taught Apollo Playes,
To his own Daphne in a stand of Bayes;
Here Myrtle Shades are, there the Cypresse Groves;
Here Lovers sigh, and there embrace their Loves:
By—through a flowry vale, there gently glides
A silver stream, whose pratling current chides

It self in Turtle-murmures, and betraid
To every eye, like to some bashful maid
Discover'd in her beauties, fain would hast
To hide those blushes which do speak her chast.
Here thy Narcissus in his lov'd despair,
Courts all the rest to silence; sweet and fair,
His love, and sorrow shews him; but to hear
Him breath 'em thus, who would not be all eare?
What in his story did before but move
Our pity, we do now admire, and love
Beyond himself; so every maid would be
His kind Nymphs Rival, borrowing from thee
Those charmes of love and language, where thy Art
Gives Cupid feathers unto every dart.
Thy Poem is as lovely, and all wit
Thy Eccho is, and making love to it:
Let Ovid boast their story, but their names
Will take Eternity from thee, dear James.

To His Learned Friend, M. James Shirley, On His Elegant Poems by Fra. Tuckyr

Friend, in this dearth of Art, when but to write
Or think in verse, is to be destroy'd quite;
When Sergeants too implacable are set
To fill the Compters up with wit and debt:
Nor any hope of rescue but from those
Who would distrust their Creed if't were not Prose,
I wonder at the influence of thy Pen,
That could ingage such generous knowing men
(Warm'd with thy flame) so boldly to advance
Gainst the prevailing monster, Ignorance.
Sure this so fair return of gratitude
To dare thus in thy cause, must needs conclude
Thy elegant expressions (while the Scene
Obey'd thy pow'rful Empire) are not clean
Obliterated, when thy all-charming wit
Secures so firm Allegiance unto it.
Tis wisely done, thus to erect a Shrine
Teternize their own names as well as thine.
I envie not their Fate; let it suffice
They deck thine Altar; but the sacrifice
Is my fixt Heart, devoted to thy worth,
Which all their labord lines can ne'er set forth.
Best Lapidaries oftentimes do set
The fairest Diamonds in a foile of Jett.

To My Very Worthy and Most Ingenious Friend, Mr. James Shirley, Upon His Poems by Ed. Powel

When I am rais'd by some more noble flame
To sing of thee, and thy Odelias Name,
So richly set in verse; Thy lines invite
Me still to read, and I forget to write.
So when a Painters hand would take the grace
And figure of some admirable face,
Struck with the sight, he lets his Pencil fall,
And when his hand should work, his eye does all.
Yet if a sence of thy sweat fancy may
Inspire a resolution to betray
My want of skill, and choise in husbandry,
To write my owne, not read thy Poetry:
Be it enough to draw the Reader neer,
While we but say the wit of Shirley's here.
And though thy worthier friends their flowers bring,
To set forth thy Odelia like the Spring,
Men will with envie look upon the dresse,
That staies their eyes from the wish'd comlinesse,
And when they see her beauty to be such,
Will say their love had shaddow'd it too much.

Amicissimo J. Sherleio, & Musae Jam Reduci by George Hill

Quid non, Te rediente, dulce sperem!
Coelorum facies nova, & novus frons
Antiquusque vigor recurrit omnis;
Nympharum proprius decor, suusque,
Fonte & Castalides suo replentur.
Dignaris mihi, caeterisque grandem
Impertire salutem, & ipse plenus
Phoebi numine, Laeta Gratiarum
Musarumque Cohors amoena, Circum
Te (Sherleie) canunt, & ore captat
Dulci Quae que tuo Jocosa Carmen.
Sic optatus eras— abibit omnis
Infoecunda & opaca nostra nubes
Te Claro rediente sole: Noster
Exul jam Genius redit; Poetam
Arridente oculo jucundus ipse
Musarum{que} suum Pater salutat.
Tendunt jam vacuam Chelyn Camoenae,

Cingit Laurea dum virens capillos:
Nectunt Coelicolae ex Tuo coronam
Horto (mellifluae Artifex Minervae)
Aptant inque Tuum Caput Sorores—
Tu illis dulce Levamen atque Amico

When th' Age groan'd out Thou and thy Must were gone,
And Epitaphs each Wit was thinking on;
When to bestrew thy grave, and stick thy Herse
With herbs, or the more fragrant flowers of Verse;
When to thy worth rich Trophies how to raise,
Our fancies strove; The Cypresse then turn'd Bayes,
Which on thy brow grac'd with Poetick Rage,
Secur'd Thee from the thunder of the Age.
Thus the Springs warmth brings back by mild degrees,
Rayment and food to th' leafelesse, saplesse Trees:
Thus the wingd quire their vocall Lutes do string,
And Turtles having found their mates, do sing:
Thus like the quickning sun, thy flames do spread,
And add new life to us, that fear'd thee dead.

Cupids Call

Ho! Cupid calls, come Lovers, come,
Bring his wanton Harvest home:
The West-wind blowes, the Birds do sing,
The Earth's enamell'd, 'tis high Spring:
Let Hinds whose soul is Corn and Hay,
Expect their crop another day.
Into Loves Spring-garden walk,
Virgins dangle on their stalk,
Full blown, and playing at fifteen:
Come bring your amorous sickles then?
See they are pointing to their beds,
And call to reap their Maiden-heads.
Hark, how in yonder shadie grove
Sweet Philomel is warbling love,
And with her voice is courting Kings,
For since she was a Bird, she sings,
There is no pleasure but in men,
Oh come and ravish me agen.
Virgins that are youg and fair
May kisse, and grow into a pair;

Then warm and active use your blood,
No sad thought congeal the flood:
Nature no med'cine can impart
When age once snows upon our heart.

To His Unkind M.

Sure thy heart was flesh at first,
For what sin hath it been curst
Into that stubborn thing of late,
Above the reach of wonder? what
In some winter was it lost,
And its blood drunk up by frost,
Grew stiffe, and so a rock became?
Yet this would soften at a flame.
Or didst thou bathe thy pretty limbs
In some cold and fatal streams,
Which turn what they embrace to stone,
And by degrees thy heart grew one?
I know not, but too true I find
A Quarry of prodigious kind:
Yet since I lov'd it, I will try
From the warm Limbeck of my eye,
In such a method to distil
Tears on thy marble nature, till
Their frequent drops by loves new Art,
Write my Epitaph on thy heart;
That men may know for whom I die,
And say beneath that stone I lie.

Good Morrow

Good morrow unto her, who in the night
Shoots from her silver brow more light
Then Cynthia, upon whose state
All other servile stars of Beauty wait.
Good morrow unto her, who gives the day,
Whose eyes preserve a purer Ray
Then Phoebus, when in Thetis streams
He hath new bath'd himself, and washt his beames.
The day and night are onely thine, and we
Were lost in darknes but for thee;
For thee we live, all hearts are thine,
But none so full of faith and flame as mine.

To His Mistris.

I would the God of Love would die,
And give his Bow and Shafts to me,
I ask no other Legacie:
This happy fate I then would prove,
That since thy heart I cannot move,
I'de cure, and kill my owne with Love.
Yet why should I so cruel be
To kill my self with loving thee,
And thou a Tyrant still to me?
Perhaps, couldst thou affection shew
To me, I should not love thee so,
And that would be my med'cine too.
Then choose to love me, or deny,
I will not be so fond to die
A Martyr to thy cruelty:
If thou bee'st weary of me, when
Thou art so wise to love agen,
Command, and I'le forsake thee then.

To Odelia.

Health to my fair Odelia, some that know
How many months are past
Since I beheld thy lovely brow,
Would count an Age at least:
But unto me
Whose thoughts are still on thee;
I vow
By thy black eyes, 'tis but an hour agoe.
That Mistris I pronounce but poor in blisse,
That when her servant parts,
Gives not as much with her last kisse,
As will maintain two hearts
Till both do meet
To taste, what else is sweet.
Is't fit
Time measure Lov, or our Affection it?
Cherish that heart Odelia, that is mine,
And if the North thou fear,
Dispatch but from thy Southern clime
A sigh, to warm thine here:

But be so kind
To send by the next wind,
'Tis far,
And many accidents do wait on War.

To His Mistris Confined

Think not my Phebe, cause a cloud
Doth now thy heavenly beauty shroud,
My wandring eye
Can stoop to common beauties of the sky.
Be thou but kind, and this Eclipse
Shall neither hinder eyes, nor lips;
For we will meet
Within our hearts, and kisse, when none shall see't.
Nor canst thou in thy Prison be,
Without some loving signes of me,
When thou dost spy
A sun-beam peep into thy room, 'tis I,
For I am hid within that flame,
And thus unto thy chamber came,
To let thee see,
In what a Martyrdom I burn for thee.
There's no sad picture that doth dwell
Upon thy Arras wall, but well
resembles me.
No matter though our yeers do not agree,
Love can make old, as well as time,
And he that doth but twenty clime,
If he will prove
As true as I, shews fourscore yeers in love.

Loves Hue and Cry

In Loves name you are charg'd, oh fly
And make a speedy Hue and Cry
After a face, which t'other day
Stole my wandring heart away:
To direct you, take in brief
These few marks to know the Thief.
Her hair a net of beams, would prove
Strong enough to imprison Jove
Drest in his Eagles shape; her brow
Is a spacious field of snow,
Her eyes so rich, so pure a gray,

Every look creates a day,
And if they close themselves (not when
The Sun doth set) 'tis night agen:
In her cheecks are to be seen
Of flowers, both the King and Queen,
Thither by all the Graces led,
And smiling in their nuptial bed:
On whom, like pretty Nymphs do wait
Her twin-born lips, whose Virgin state
They do deplore themselves, nor misse
To blush, so often as they kisse
Without a Man. Beside the rest,
You shall know this fellon best
By her tongue, for when your ear
Once a harmonie shall hear
So ravishing, you do not know
Whether you be in heaven, or no;
That, that is she; O straight surprize,
And bring her unto Loves Assize;
But lose no time, for fear that she
Ruine all mankind, like me,
Fate, and Philosophy controul,
And leave the world without a soul.

Goodnight

Bid me no more goodnight; because
'Tis dark, must I away?
Love doth acknowledge no such Lawes,
And Love 'tis I obey:
Which blind, doth all your light despise,
And hath no need of eyes
When day is fled:
Besides the Sun, which you
Complain is gone, 'tis true,
Is gone to bed:
Oh let us do so too.

Would you know what's soft? I dare
Remit you to the Down, or Ayre:
The Stars we all acknowledge bright,
The Snow too is exceeding white:
To please your sent, 't will not be hard
To present you bruised Nard:
And would you heavenly musick hear,
I'le call the Orbes to take your ear,

If old Pythagoras sing true.
But Ambrosia, heavenly dew
Divinely must affect your taste,
And Nectar is your drink at last.
But would you have all these delights in one,
Know but the fair Odelia, and 'tis done,

A Fayring

A Fayring if you ask, I will next day
Bestow upon you the new puppet play:
The children made in wax, I dare not try,
For I confesse, the modells at your eye
Will melt themselves away, and then you know
The man will be undone, and lose his show.
What monsters would you see? Ile bring a man
Has been in France or Italy, that can
Play his deformities with all the fair.
Wee'l for the Cloysters, where the pictures are,
The King and Queens, the Princes, all the babies,
The paper Lords, and all the painted Ladies,
The men of ginger-bread, what art can do,
You shall see Canibals will eat them too.
Wee'l to the horse that dances, and ('tis said)
Tells money and which Virgin is a maid.
This beast must be an understanding creature,
For he will snort you by instinct of nature:
If you but name the Pope, there's somthing in't,
That a wall eye should read Geneva print.
These are but half the knacks wee'l see, and buy,
If you will walk into the Fayr with me:
But you are angry, Mistris, troth, I meant
A jest, in answer of your merriment;
For sure you cannot mean, with hope to gain
That gift from me is worth your entertain.
For whatsoever is not I, must be
Trifles, and empty things bestow'd on thee;
And you may thank your beauty for't, I am
So poor, I have not left my self a name,
Or substance, not translated thine before,
He that bestow'd his heart, can give no more.
If thou wilt have a Fayring from me, then
Give my self back, Ile give it thee agen.

To L. for a Wreath of Bayes Sent

Soul of my Muse! what active unknown fire
Already doth thy Delphick wreath inspire?
O'th sudden, how my faculties swell high,
And I am all a powerful Prophesie!
Sleep ye dull Caesars, Rome will boast in vain
Your glorious Tryumphs, One is in my brain,
Great as all yours, and circled with thy Bayes,
My thoughts take Empire o're all land and seas:
Proof against all the Planets, and the stroke
Of Thunder, I rise up Augustus Oake
Within my guard of Laurel, and made free
From age, look fresh still as my Daphnean Tree.
My Fancie's narrow yet, till I create
For thee another world, and in a state
As free as Innocence, shame all Poets wit,
To climb no higher then Elizium yet,
Where the pale lovers meet, and teach the groves
To sigh, and sing vain legends of their loves;
We will have other flights, and raste such things
Are onely fit for Sainted Queens and Kings.
Musaeus, Homer, and ye sacred rest,
Long since beleev'd in your own ashes blest,
Awake, and live again, and having wrote
Our story, wish your other songs forgot,
And your selves too, but our high Subject must
In spite of death and time, new soul your dust.
What cannot I command? what can a thought
Be now ambitious of, but shall be brought
By vertue of my charme? I will undo
The yeer, and at my pleasure make one new:
All Spring, whose blooming Paradise, but when
I list, shall with one frown wither agen.
Astrologers leave searching the vast skies,
Teach them all fate, Odelia, from thine eyes;
All that was earth resolves, my spirit's free,
I have nothing left now but my Soul and Thee.

To the Painter Preparing to Draw M. M. H.

Be not too forward Painter: 'tis
More for thy fame, and art, to misse
All other faces, then come neer
The Lady, that expecteth here:
Be wise, and think it lesse disgrace

To draw an Angel, then her face:
For in such formes, who is so wise
To tell thee where thy error lies?
But since all beauty (that is known)
Is in her Virgin sweetnes, One,
How can it be, that painting her,
But every look should make thee erre?
But thou art resolute I see;
Yet let my fancy walk with thee:
Compose a ground more dark and sad,
Then that the early Chaos had:
And shew, to the whole Sexes shame,
Beauty was darknes till she came:
Then paint her eyes, whose active light
Shall make the former shadows bright:
And with their every beam supply
New day, to draw her picture by:
Now, if thou wilt compleat the face,
A wonder paint in every place.
Beneath these, for her fair necks sake,
White, as the Paphian Turtles, make
A pillar, whose smooth base doth show
It self lost in a mount of snow:
Her brest, the house of chast desire,
Cold, but increasing others fire.
But how I lose (instructing thee)
Thy pencil, and my Poetry?
For when thou hast exprest all art,
As high as truth, in every part,
She can resemble at the best,
One, in her beauties silence drest,
Where thou, like a dull looker on,
Art lost, and all thy art undone:
For if she speak, new wonders rise
From her teeth, chin, lip, and eyes:
So far above that excellent
Did take thee first, thou wo't repent
To have begun, and lose i'th' end
Thy eyes with wonder how to mend.
At such a losse, here's all thy choice,
Leave off, or paint her with a voice.

To a L. Who Had Courted a Lady of Much Perfection, and After Offered His Service to Another of an Inferiour Beauty and Parts; in Confidence that the First Would Re-accept Him.

And can thy proud Apostate eyes

Court her again, with hope t' entice
One gentle language, or a smile
Upon a Renegade so vile?
Thing call'd a Lord, forbear; 'tis fit
Ambition leave thee like thy wit.
Send for an Exorcist from Rome,
And let him with full orders come,
To dispossesse thy wanton sence
Of this grand divel, Impudence.
Can she, in whom shines every grace,
Loves wide fancy can embrace,
Forget her nobler soul, to be
Upon thy pride retriv'd by thee?
She hath let fall too many beams;
Thus heaven upon corrupted streams
Hath dropp'd transparent dew, which shewes
The Spring is cleer, whence crystal flowes.
Enjoy thy madnes, or what's worse,
Thy new made Mistris, 'tis a curse
To be in hell, but thine is more,
Whose eyes have witnest heaven before:
Th' Hesperian apples thou maist see
Hereafter, but ne'er climb the tree;
For rather then thou gather fruit,
The Plant will wither at the root.
Dote still upon the Dragon, she
Is fierce, and form'd enough for thee:
And if thy owne ill can dispence,
Kisse there, and suck more poyson thence.

A Lover That Durst Not Speak to His M.

I can no longer hold, my body growes
Too narrow for my soul, sick with repose,
My passions call to be abroad; and where
Should I discharge their weight, but in her ear,
From whose fair eyes the burning arrow came,
And made my heart the Trophie to her flame.
I dare not. How? Cupid is blind we know,
I never heard that he was dumb till now;
Love, and not tell my Mistris? How crept in
That subtle shaft? Is it to love a sin?
Is't ill to feed a longing in my blood?
And was't no fault in her to be so good?
I must not then be silent, yet forbear,
Convey thy passion rather in some tear,

Or let a sigh expresse, how much thy blisse
Depends on her, or breathe it in a kisse,
And mingle souls; loud accents call the eyes
Of envie, and but waken jealousies:
Then silence be my language, which if she
But understand, and speak again to me,
We shall secure our Fate, and prove at least
The miracles of love are not quite ceast.
Bar frowns from our discourse, and ev'ry where
A smile may be his owne Interpreter.
Thus we may read in spite of standers by,
Whole volumes, in the twinckling of an eye.

To One That Said His Mistris Was Old

Tell me not Time hath plaid the Thief
Upon her beauty, my belief
Might have been mock'd, and I had been
An Heretick, if I had not seen,
My Mistris is still fair to me,
And now I all those graces see
That did adorn her Virgin brow;
Her eye hath the same flame in't now,
To kill or save, the Chymists fire
Equally burns; so my desire:
Not any Rose-bud lesse within
Her cheek, the same snow on her chin:
Her voice that heavenly musick bears,
First charm'd my soul, and in my eares
Did leave it trembling, her lips are
The self same lovely Twinnes they were:
After so many yeers I misse
No Flower in all my Paradise.
Time, I despise thy rage, and thee,
Theeves do not alwaies thrive, I see.

Upon His M. Dancing

I Stood and saw my Mistris dance,
Silent, and with so fixt an eye,
Some might suppose me in a trance,
But being asked why,
By one that knew I was in love,
I could not but impart

My wonder, to behold her move
So nimbly with a marble heart.

Upon His Mistris Sad

Melancholy hence, and get
Some peece of earth to be thy seat,
Here the Ayre and nimble fire
Would shoot up to meet desire;
Sullen humor leave her blood,
Mixe not with the purer Flood,
But let pleasures swelling here,
Make a Spring-tide all the yeer.
Love a thousand sweets distilling,
And with pleasure bosomes filling,
Charm all eyes, that none may find us,
Be above, before, behind us:
And while we thy raptures taste,
Compel time it self to stay,
Or by forelock hold him fast,
Least occasion slip away.

A Gentleman in Love with Two Ladies

If Love his arrowes shoot so fast,
Soon his feather'd stock will waste,
But I mistake in thinking so:
Loves arrowes in his quiver grow;
And it appears too true in me,
Cupid wants no Artillery,
Two shafts feed upon my brest,
Make it a mark for all the rest:
Kill me with love, thou angry Sun
Of Citherea, or let one,
But one sharp golden Arrow flie.
To wound that heart for whom I die.
Cupid if thou bee'st a child,
Be no god, or be more mild.

Melancholy Converted

Welcom, welcom again to thy wits,

This is a Holy-day;
Wee'l have no plots, nor melancholy fits,
But merrily passe the time away.
They are mad that are sad;
Be rul'd by me,
And never were two so merry as we.
The kitchin shall catch cold no more,
Wee'l have no key to the buttry dore,
The Fidlers shall sing,
The house shall ring,
And the World shall see
What a merry merry couple we will be.

To a Mistris in Whose Letter Some Tears Were Dropt

Think not my dearest Mistris, that I can
Forget my vows to thee, and be a man:
Love is for more then life, that's but a span.
Those drops which on thy Letter did appear,
At once both stain'd and made thy paper clear,
I would have read thy eyes, and not thy tear.
Yet Ile not chide thee for it, it may be
To make me rich thou sentst those pearls to me:
Alas, I must be poor in wanting thee.
Had I a thought about me did not lay
Thee up a treasure to my love, Ide say
Thy tears were sorrow for my sin, and pray.
But knowing my selfe thine, how e're thou do
An act to grieve my love, and thy owne too,
My self Ile flatter by not thinking so.
Examine thy own soul, and if thou find
Faith there, it was but coppyed from my mind;
Which may be wounded, never be unkind.
So farewel my Odelia, be thou just,
For when I die, I'le love thee in my dust;
And when I fail thee most, secure thy trust.

Presenting His Mistris with a Bird

Walking to taste the welcom Spring,
The Birds which cheerful notes did sing
On their green Perches, 'mong the rest,
One whose sweet warble pleas'd me best,
I tempted to the snare, and caught,

To you I send it to be taught;
'Tis young, and apt to learn, and neer
A voice so full of art, and cleer
As yours, it cannot choose but rise
Quickly a Bird of Paradise.

Upon Scarlet and Blush Coloured Ribbands Given by Two Ladies

Let other servants boast a snowy glove,
Or glory in their Mistris hair,
Or think they straight immortal prove
If they once obtain to wear
A Ring enamell'd, by her finger blest,
Wherein the Rainbow is exprest,
In whose circle Cupid dwelling,
Doth offer a sweet Poesie to their smelling.
Not all the orient beauties that embrace
Fair Venus neck, nay grant that she
Daigne to disfurnish her own face,
And bestow her Mole on me:
Not this, nor those are half so rich, so fair
As these two silken Ribbands are;
Favours Juno might have given
The Graces, on her wedding day in heaven.
Mysterious Colours! carrying more then show,
For you expresse in your rich dye
Rare vertues, which the givers owe,
Constant love, and modesty:
To which when I prove false, my blood be curst,
To satisfie the injur'd first:
Shame be next reward, and then
I forfeit Blush, and Scarlet back agen.

To His Mistris Upon the Bayes Withered

Fair Cruel, see the Bayes which thou
Didst send to crown my verse:
How well with Cypresse, and sad Ewe
Would it become my herse?
'Tis thy unkindnes that doth kill
The leaves, which fade like me,
Yet on the wreath but cast a smile,
'Twill seem another Tree.
Such shine will quicken what is dead,

Then send it me agen,
Which shall have vertue on my head,
To make the wearer green.
Thus in a frost I'le meet a flame,
And Phoebus Priest am made,
And Thee, I growing fresh, will name
My Nymph, my light, my shade.

Strephon, Daphne

Strephon
Come my Daphne, come away,
We do waste the Crystal day;
'Tis Strephon calls.

Daphne
What would my love?

Strephon
Come follow to the Mirtle grove;
Where Venus shall prepare
New chaplets for thy hair.

Daphne
Were I shut up within a tree,
Ide rend my bark to follow thee.

Strephon
My shepherdesse, make haste,
The minutes slide too fast:

Daphne
In those cooler shades will I
Blind, as Cupid, kisse thine eye.

Strephon
In thy perfumed bosome then Ile stray,
In such warm snow who would not lose his way?

Chorus
Wee'l laugh and leave this world behind,
And gods themselves that see,
Shall envie thee, and me:
But never find
Such joyes, when they embrace a Deity.

Taking Leave When His Mistris Was to Ride

How is it my ungentle fate,
When Love commanded me to wait
Upon my Saint, by break of day,
I brought a heart, but carried none away?
When we joyn'd ceremonious breath,
And lips, that took a leave like death,
With a sad parting thought opprest,
Did it leave mine, to glide into her brest?
Or was it when like Pallas she
Was mounted, and I gaz'd to see,
My heart then looking through mine eye,
Did after her out at that window flie?
'Twas so, and cause I did not ride,
My heart would Lackey by her side,
Or some more careful Angel be,
To see my Mistris safe convey'd for me.
Nay then attend thy charge, nor fear
Storms in the way, and if a tear
By chance, at looking back on thee
Bedew her eye, drink that a health to me.
But smile at night, and be her guest,
At once her musick and her feast,
And if at any mention made
Of me, she sigh, say all thy travell's paid.
But when shee's gently laid to rest,
Oh listen softly to her brest,
And thou shalt hear her soul, but see
Thou wake her not, for she may dream of me.
But what's all this, when I am here,
If fancie bid thee welcom there?
Heart, this last dutie I implore,
Or bring her back, or see thy Cell no more.

Love for Enjoying

Fair Lady, what's your face to me?
I was not onely made to see,
Every silent stander by
May thus enjoy as much as I.
That blooming nature on your cheek,
Is still inviting me to seek
For unknown wealth, within the ground

Are all the Royal mettals found,
Leave me to search, I have a thread
Through all the Labyrinth shall lead,
And through every winding veine
Conduct me to the golden Mine;
Which once enjoy'd, will give me power
To make new Indies every houre:
Look on those Jewells that abound
Upon your dresse, that Diamond
No flame, no lustre could impart,
Should not the Lapidaries Art
Contribute here and there a star,
And just such things ye women are,
Who do not in rude Quarries shine,
But meeting us y'are made divine.
Come let us mixe our selves, and prove
That action is the soul of Love;
Why do we coward-gazing stand,
Like Armies in the Netherland,
Contracting fear at eithers sight,
Till we both grow too weak to fight?
Let's charge for shame, and chuse you whether
One shall fall, or both together;
This is Loves war, who ever dies,
If the surviver be but wise,
He may reduce the spirit fled,
For t'other kisse will cure the dead.

Upon the Princes Birth

Fair fall the Muses that in well-chim'd verse
Our Princes happy birth do sing,
I have a heart as full of joy as their's,
As full of duty to my King,
And thus I tell
How every bell
Did ring forth Englands merry glee,
The Bonefires too,
With much adoe
It were great pity to belye her,
Made all the City seem one fire,
A joyful sight to see.
The graver Citizens were foxt that day,
With beer and joy most soundly paid,
The Constables in duty reeld away,
And charged others them to aid:

To see how soon
Both Sun and Moon,
And the seven Stars forgotten be;
But when 'twas night
Their heads were light,
To which they did exalt their horn,
Because a Prince of Wales was born:
A joyful &c.
The Dutch-men having drunk so much before,
Could not so well expresse their joy:
The French condemn'd not to be sober more,
Drank healths unto the Royal Boy,
In their own wine,
Neat, brisk, and fine:
The valiant Irish, Cram-a-Cree,
It pledged hath
In Usquebagh,
And being in this jovial vein,
They made a bogg even of their brain,
A joyful &c.
The Welsh for joy her Cosin Prince was born,
Was mean to change S. Tavie's day,
Swearing no leeks was be hereafter worn
But on the twenty nine of May:
None so merry
Drinking Perry,
And Metheglin on their knee;
Was every man
A Trojan than;
Thus arm'd the Tivel her defie,
And dare tell Beelzebub her lie.
A joyful &c.
The Scots in bonny ale their joy did sing,
And wish'd the Royal Babe a man
That they might beg him but to be their King,
And let him rule' em when he can:
The Spanjard made
A shrugg, and said
After my pipe, come follow me,
Canary Sack
Did go to wrack,
Some Marchants went to Malago,
Some drown'd in good old Charnico,
A joyful &c.
And now let all good Subjects prayers ascend,
That heaven with milk would swel their brest
That nurse the babe, may Angels still attend
To rock him gently to his rest.

Let his glory
Raise a story
Worthy an immortal pen:
So Charles God blesse,
Our Queen no lesse,
And in conclusion of my Song,
I wish that man without a tongue
That will not say Amen.

To His Honoured Friend Thomas Stanley Esquire, Upon His Elegant Poems

A Palsie shakes my pen, while I intend
A votive to thy Muse; since to commend
With my best skill, will be as short of thee,
As thou above all future poesie.
Thou early miracle of Wit and Art,
That hath prodigiously so got the start
Of Ages in thy study; Time must be
Old once agen in overtaking thee.
I know not where I am, when I peruse
Thy learned loves, how willingly I lose
My self in every grove? and wish to be
(Might it contribute to thy wreath) a Tree,
Carew, whose numerous language did before
Steer every genial soul, must be no more
The Oracle of Love, and might he come
But from his own to thy Elizium,
He would repent his immortality
Given by loose Idolaters, and die
A Tenant to these shades, and by thy ray
He need not blush to court his Celia.
Thy numbers carry height, yet cleer, and terse,
And innocent, as becomes the soul of verse:
Poets from hence may add to their great name,
And learn to strike from Chastity a flame.
But I expect some murmuring Critick here
Should say, no Poems ever did appear
Without some fault, this I must grant a truth,
And Sir, let me deal plainly with your youth,
Not error-proof yet, somthing may admit
A censure, if you will secure your wit,
I know the onely way to bring't about,
Accept my love, and leave this coppy out.

To the E. of S. Upon His Recovery

My Lord, the voice that did your sicknes tell,
Strook like a midnight chime or knell;
At every sound
I took into my sence a wound,
Which had no cure till I did hear
Your health agen
Restor'd, and then
There was a balsame powr'd into mine ear.
It was my wonder first, what could invade
A temper was so even made;
Then fear stept in,
Lest nature should commit a sin
By yeelding to resigne your breath,
Upon whose herse
All tears and verse
Would fall, but not enough lament your death.
But hymnes are now requir'd, 'tis time to rise,
And pay the altar sacrifice,
My heart allowes
No gummes, nor amber, but pure vowes,
There's fire at breathing of your name,
And do not fear,
I have a tear
Of joy, to curb any immodest flame.
In you, since honour is restor'd, oh may
Health in your noble bosome stay,
And with your blood
Move in a Circle all that's good;
And though Time sicken with his yeers,
And winter's come,
Let your Age bloome,
And look as fresh as when the Spring appears.

One That Loved None but Deformed Women

What should my Mistris do with hair?
Her frizling, curling, I can spare;
But let her forehead be well plough'd,
And Hempe within the furrowes sow'd.
No dressing should conceal her ear,
Which I would have at length appear,
At which should hang with a device,
The wealthy pearls of both her eyes.
And such a Nose I would desire

Should represent the Town a fire;
Cheeks black, and swelling like the south,
No tongue, nor mark within her mouth.
Oh give me such a face,
Such a grace,
No two should have sport,
Or in wedlock better agree:
The divel should into the bawdy Court
If he durst but Cuckold me.

The Common-Wealth of Birds

Let other Poets write of dogs,
Some sing of fleas, or fighting frogs,
Anothers Muse be catching fish,
And every Bird cook his owne dish.
The Common-wealth of Birds I bring
To feast your eares: then hear me sing.
A Buzzard is the Major o'th' Town,
And Gulls are Brethren of the Gown,
Some Widgens of the Peace and Quorum,
Commit all that are brought before um.
Cocks are the under-men of trade,
Within whose Hall a Law is made,
That every Spring each Citizen
Shall march, to bring the Cuckoe in.
Every Constable has a claw,
A head of Batt, and brain of Daw;
And as wife as these, you will
Know the Watchmen by their bill;
Who take no wandring Owles by night
But they convey them to the Kite
Who keeps the Compter, where together
They laugh, and drink, and molt their feather.
If you come to Court, there are
A Robin Red-brest, and a Stare;
Canary Birds do sigh, not sing,
The Larks have quite forgot the Spring.
What should harmonious birds sing there,
When a Rook's master of the Quire?
They that do practise Common-pleas
With greatest art, are Goldfinches:
And Crowes by Physick, plump, and thrive,
Men die, that birds of prey may live.
If for the Church you look, sad age!
You'l find the Clergie in a Cage:

Faith and Religion declines,
When good wits are no more Divines:
For Lapwings every-where you'l see
Perch up, and preach Divinitie;
Who sing, though every soul be vext,
Here 'tis, when farthest from their Text.
But what most admiration moves,
The souldiers are all fighting Doves;
And no reward for Prose, or Verse,
The Scholars are turn'd wood-peckers.
So fast the various birds intrude,
Art cannot name them; To conclude,
Every wise-marris a VVren,
And black-Swans the honest men.
A wonder in the close I bring,
A Nightingale to these is King,
Who never (sweet Bird) goes to rest,
But has a Thorne upon his brest.

To the Excellent Pattern of Beauty and Vertue, L. El. Co. of Or.

Madam,
Were you but onely great, there are some men
Whose heat is not the Muses, nor their Pen
Steer'd by chast truth, could flatter you in prose,
Or glorious verse, but I am none of those:
I never learn'd that trick of Court to wear
Silk at the cost of flatt'ry, or make dear
My pride, by painting a great Ladies face
When she had don't before, and swear the grace
Was Natures; Anagram upon her Name,
And add to her no vertue, my owne shame.
I could not make this Lord a god, then try
How to commit new Court idolatry;
And when he dies, hang on his silent herse
Wet Elegies, and haunt his ghost in verse:
These, some hold witty, thriving garbs; but I
Choose to my losse a modest Poesie;
And place my Genius upon Subjects fit
For imitation rather then bold wit;
And such are you, who both in name and blood
Born great, have learn'd this lesson to be good.
Arm'd with this knowledge, Madam, I not fear
To hold fair correspondence with the year,
And bring my gift, hearty, as you are fair,
A servants wish, for all my wealth is prayer,

Which with the yeer thus enters. May you be
Still the same flowing goodnes that we see.
In your most noble Lord be happy still,
And heaven chain your hearts into one will!
Be rich in your two darlings of the Spring,
Which as it waits, perfumes their blossoming,
The growing pledges of your love, and blood;
And may that unborn blessing timely bud,
The chast, and noble Treasure of your womb,
Your owne, and th'Ages expectation come!
And when your daies and vertues have made even,
Die late, belov'd of earth, and change for heaven.

To the H. Lady, D. C. at His Departure

Madam whose first stile is good,
Great in vertue as in blood,
For my entertainment, take
This warm sacrifice, I make
In wishes, which flow best, which art
Hath little traffick with the heart.
May every Sun that rises, pay
You pleasure long liv'd as the day,
And at night the silent streams
Of pious thoughts fill up your dreams:
For him, to whom your heart is tyed,
Keep it still Virgin, and Bride,
That often as you go to bed,
You give and take a maiden-head.
Never sigh, but when you pray,
May your Husband smile all day:
And when clouds make dark his skie,
Strike new day-light from your eye,
And if e're he think amisse,
May you cure him with a kisse!
But to keep his heart at home,
Be rich in treasures of your womb,
And taught by examples of your love,
With every Olive-branch a Dove.

A Letter to the Lady D. S. Sent with a New Comedy.

Madam, who make the glory of your blood
No priviledge at all to be lesse good;

Pardon the rudenes of a Comedy,
That (taught too great ambition) would flie
To kisse your white hand, and receive from thence,
Both an authority, and innocence.
'Tis not this great man, nor this Prince, whose fame
Can more advance a Poem, then your name,
To whose dear vertue truth is bound, and we,
That there is so much left for history.
I do acknowledge custom, that to men
Such Poems are presented, but my pen
Is not engaged, nor can allow too far
A Salique law in Poetry, to bar
Ladies th'inheritance of wit, whose soul
It active, and not able to controul,
At some usurp the chair, which write a stile
To breathe the Reader better then a mile;
But no such empty titles buy my flame,
Nor will I sin so much to shew their name
In print; some servile Muses be their drudge,
That sweat to find a Patron, not a Judge.
To you great Lady then, in whom do meet
Candor and Judgement, humble at your feet
I throw these papers, wishing you may see
Joyes multiplyed, to your eternity.

To the Never Enough Honoured E. of St. on New Yeares Day at Night, After Other Entertainment

SIr, give me leave to Court your stay,
There is somthing I must pay,
Due to your greatnesse, and the day,
Which by a revolution of the Sphere
Is proud to open the New-year,
And having look'd on you, hath hid his face,
And chang'd his robe, with stars to grace
And light you going to bed, so wait
With trembling lustre on your state.
Shine brighter yet, y are not the same,
Cleer Lamps you were, shine like the name
Of him I bow to, while a flame
Active and burning here with pure desires,
Shall equal your best borrow'd fires.
May health, the bosoms friend stream through your blood
And know no end of the chast flood:
And though time shift, and yeers renew,
May yet the Spring be still in you.
May she, whom heaven hath sweetly grac'd

And in your noble bosome plac'd,
Whose heart, by onely you embrac'd
Hath made one true, and holy Gordian prove
Fruitful in children as in love:
And may that fair top branch, whose early bloom
Doth promise all the fruit can come
To vertue, and your name, be blest,
And live a story to the rest.
All honour with your same increase,
In your bosome dwell soft peace,
And Justice the true root of these.
Wealth be the worst, and outside of your fate,
And may not heav'n your life translate,
Till for your Royal Master, and this Isle.
Your acts have fill'd a Chronicle.
In all that's great and good, be bold,
And every yeer be coppy of the old.

To W. M. of N.

Hail great Preserver of the King
And your owne honour; such a thing
At Court but rare appears;
And when in calmer years
So much vertue, so much crime
Shall be read both at one time:
Treason shall want a Child, and your worth knowne,
Posterity shall thank the Kingdoms grone.
When I before did fancy Men
Of a most glorious soul, my pen
Did Prophesie of you,
To whom so much is due,
That each Patriot must rise
To court you with a sacrifice,
And boldest Writers telling ages, why
Need fear no fiction in their Poetry.
Great both in Peace and War, thus fame
Did honour Sidney; on your name
Two Laurels grew, and they
That speak them both, may say,
Thus the fluent Ovid wrote,
And thus too, wise Caesar fought;
For when your story shall be perfect, you
May both deserve, and have their envies too.

To M. Phil. Massenger on His Renegado

Dablers in Poetry, that onely can
Court this weak Lady, or that Gentleman
With some loose wit in time;
Others that fright the time
Into belief with mighty words, that tear
A passage through the ear;
Or nicer men
That through a perspective will see a play,
And use it the wrong way,
(Not worth thy pen)
Though all their pride exalt them, cannot be
Competent Judges of thy lines or thee.
I must confesse I have no glorious name
To rescue judgement, no Poetick flame
To dresse thy Muse with praise,
And Phoebus his owne bayes;
Yet I commend this Poem, and dare tell
The World I lik't it well;
And if there be
A Tribe, who in their wisdom dare accuse
The Off-spring of thy Muse;
Let them agree,
Conspire one Comedie, and they will say
'Tis easier to commend then make a Play.

Io.

You Virgins that did late despair
To keep your wealth from cruel men,
Tye up in silk your eareles hair,
Soft peace is come agen.
Now Lovers eyes may gentle shoot
A flame that wo'not kill:
The Drum was angry, but the Lute
Shall whisper what you will.
Sing Io, Io, for his sake,
Who hath restor'd your drooping heads,
With choice of sweetest flowers make
A garden where he treads.
Whil'st we whole groves of Laurel bring,
A petty triumph to his brow,
Who is the Master of our Spring,
And all the bloom we owe.

To a L. Upon a Looking-Glasse Sent

When this Crystal shall present
Your beauty to your eye,
Think that lovely face was meant
To dresse another by.
For not to make them proud
These glasses are allow'd
To those are faire,
But to compare
The inward beauty with the outward grace,
And make them fair in soul as well as face.

A Song in a Play Called Hide-Parke

I.
Come Muses all that dwel nigh the fountain,
Made by the winged horses heel,
Which firked with his Rider over each mountain,
Let me your galloping raptures feel:
I do not sing of fleas or frogs,
Nor of the well mouthed hunting dogs;
Let me be just, all praises must
Be given to the wel-breath'd lilian thrust.

II.
Young Constable and kill Deers famous,
The Cat, the Mouse, and Noddy Gray,
With nimble Pegabrig you cannot shame us
With Spanjard nor with Spinola:
Hill climbing whit-erose, praise doth not lack,
Handsome Dunbar, and yellow Jack:
But if I be just, all praises must
Be given to the well-breathed lilian thrust.

III.
Sure spurred sloven, true running Robin,
Of young Shaver I do not say lesse,
Strawberry Some, and let Spider pop in,
Fine Bruckly and brave lurching Besse,
Victorious too was Herring Shotten,
And spit in his Arse was not forgotten,
But if I be just, all honour must
Be given to well breathed lilian thrust.

IV.
Lusty George, and Gentleman hark yet,
To wining Mackarel, fine mouthed Freak,
Bay Tarral that won the cup at New-market,
Thundring tempest, black dragon eak,
Precious sweetlips I do not lose,
Nor Tobie with his golden shooes;
But if I be just, all honour must
Be given to well-breathed lilian thrust.

Epithalamium

I.
Oh look anon, if in the seeded sky
You misse no stars, here I did spy
Two gliding by.

II.
Did not thy trembling sence mistake the shine?
Which from the flaming marriage Pine
Shot like divine.

I.
No, no, oh no, within his stock of light
Hymen was never half so bright;

II.
Behold the Nuptial Train
Come smiling back again;
Hymen, hold up thy Torch.

I.
Now, now I see
The Virgin Bride, fair Willoughby,
From whose fair eyes
This day did rise,

II.
Whilst her chast blushing strowes
Fresh Roses on the morning as she goes.

I.
What Musick have they?

II.

None,
But what's the Bridegroomes owne:
See where he follows to supply
All that a well tun'd ear
Can wish to hear,
Being himself a walking Harmony.

Chorus.
HEaven on this Payr drop all the joyes
Of Love, Health, Fortune, Pleasure, Boyes.

A Mother Hearing Her Child was Sick of the Small-Poxe

What hath my pretty child misdone?
That heaven so soon,
(As if it did repent
The sweetnes it had lent)
Making so many graves, mistook the place,
And buryed all her beauty in her face.
But it foresaw if she remain'd
Fresh and unstain'd,
So blooming in each part,
She might take every heart,
Charme all the Muses to forget their verse,
Or name no beauty in their song, but hers.
But this is still my sorrow child,
With which turn'd wild,
I send my tears to seek,
And bathe thy withered cheek:
Which could my kisses reach, with warm supplies,
I would leave thee no spots, or me no eyes.

Epithalamium. To His Noble Friend, Mr. I. W.

Adorn the Altar, many come to day
To sacrifice:
But first upon't let me presume to lay
My grain of Spice;
'Tis all I have, though others bring
Rich gifts, mine is the offering.
Live one in heart so long, till time forget
You have been two,
Upon your bosomes, Joyes more frequent sit
Then Pearls of dew

On the green check of earth, but may
No Sun kisse one of these away.
Plenty your Tables, chast desires still meet
To crown your beds;
And may the Bridegroom the first night beget
New Maidenheads.
I could say more, but Verse ir tyed,
Wild Joyes in Prose are best supply'd.

A Catch

Come let us throw the dice who shall drink,
Mine is {:::} {:::} and his {:::} {:·:}
{:::} and {::} is a cast, {:::} and {`·.} not too fast,
Come aloft {:·:} {`·.}, {:::} {·} fair Play.
{::} {`.} is your throw sir, {::} {·} they run low sir
{`.} {`.} we see {`.} {·} is but three,
Oh where is the Wine, come fill up his glasse,
For here is the man that has thrown {·} {·}.

On a Black Ribband

Though Love, and Honour take a pride to dresse
Their servants in these silken liveries,
But choose the colours alwaies gay, and bright,
Excluding black, as the dark child of night,
(Which constant to its own complexion, knows
Not how to blush, nor one Indulgence owes
Either to Beauty, or the gift of Kings,
This Jealousie, and that vexation brings)
Give me the black embracement on my arme,
Which like a potent Amulet, or Charme,
Shall countermand all Magick, and defie
The smiles of love, and snares of Majesty.
Of this, I'le be more proud, then when the fair
Odelia once gave me her wreath of hair,
Wherin, her fingers taught by love, had wrought
A Net, to catch, and hold each subtle thought.
This mourning bracelet is to me above
All Ribbands, which the Robinhoods of love
Are trickt withall, who but present at Court
Which are the Race-nags for the Ladies sport.
Give me that sable Ornament, that may
Vye honour with the Nova Scotia:

Or Crimson Bath; and still reserv'd to'th' King
My reverence, who is the soul, and spring
Of English Honour, for the Garters sake,
I should not mourn, although the blue were black,
And 'tis within his brest, when Charles will please
To create one of black, to outshine these,
For what bold Antiquaries will deny,
Of Colours, Sable the first Heraldry?
All Orders have their growth, and this, when sent
To me, had somthing that was glorious meant,
From One, whose blood writes noble, but his mind
And souls extraction leave that stream behind:
And this who knowes in calmer time may thrive,
And grow into a Name, if Arts survive?
Till when, to this black Arme-let, it shall be
My Honour to be call'd a Votary.

To Gent. That Broke Their Promise of a Meeting, Made When They Drank Claret

There is no Faith in Claret, and it shall
Henceforth with me be held Apocryphal.
Ile trust a small-beer promise, nay a Troth
Wash'd in the Thames, before a french wine oath.
That Grape, they say is binding; yes, 'tis so,
And it has made your souls thus costive too.
Circe transform'd the Greeks, no hard designe,
For some can do as much with Claret wine
Upon themselves, witnes you two, allow'd
Once honest, now turn'd Ayre, and A-la-mode.
Begin no health in this, or if by chance
The Kings, 'twill question your allegiance;
And men will after all your rufling, say,
You drink as some do fight, in the French way;
Engage and trouble many, when 'tis known,
You spread their interest to wave your owne.
Away with this false Christian, it shall be
An excommunicate from mirth, and me;
Give me the Catholique diviner flame,
To light me to the fair Odelias Name:
'Tis Sack that justifies both man and verse,
Whilst you in Lethe-Claret still converse.
Forget your owne names next, and when you look
With hope to find, be lost in the Church-book.

Upon a Gentlewoman That Died of a Fever

Death, time, and sicknes, had been many a day
Conspiring this sweet Virgin to betray;
At last impatient, vow'd e're the next Sun,
To finish what their malice had begun.
Sicknes went slowly on, but time, apace,
Death lag'd behind, by night all reacht the place.
But when resolv'd of a surprize, they came,
They found her guarded by a holy flame
Her waking Fever kept, this did affright
The theeves, who are still fearful of the light.
Time stayes without; but sicknes, by the sin
Of bribing a false servant, was let in:
Death follow'd the advantage, and did creep
Into her chamber, where though in her sleep,
Sicknes faint-hearted could not stop her breath,
But she soon found the Icie hand of death.
Her grone awak'd some friends, and the maid kild,
With sighes, and clamors all the ayre was fill'd
Fearing a swift pursuite, Time ran away,
Sicknes no longer had the heart to stay,
Death with his prey soon hid him under ground,
Not since by any living creature found.

Upon the Death of G. M.

I Lov'd him, and I lost him too, then why
Should others weep their farewel, and not I?
If souls know more by being body free,
He'l know from all the rest, these drops from me.
Then flow apace, I see where store of rain
Is met, and swoln it self into a Main,
Go lose your selves in that, it cannot be
In vain, to add some water to the Sea,
Since heaven, whose glorious Constellations are
So many, hath yet took another Star.
If any think my grief has but a face
Of mourning, and my tears a common place.
Be judg your selves, that know what 'tis to leave
A friend, then wisely teach me how to grieve:
Be judge you that did want him, while he liv'd,
But more now, since he then your lives repriv'd,
Forfeit to miseries, and let me know
What height and method you'l prescribe your wo!
Be judge that were companions of his wit,

And knew with what wise Art he manag'd it.
When Natures darling bleeds, who can be found
Whose heart would not drop balme into the wound?
Last be you Judges, who best teach the way,
And steer our erring souls to heaven, then say
How much Divinity is gone, and by
Your grief Ile learn to write his Elegie.

Upon the Death of King James

When busie Fame was almost out of breath,
With telling to the world King James his death,
I gave the voice no credit; not that I
Beleev'd in Law, That Kings can never die:
For though of purer mold, at last they must
Resolve to their cold principle, the dust,
Distinguish'd onely from the common men,
That being dead, their dust is Royal then.
What though the King were old? as soon must they
Be at home, whose journey's down-hill all the way.
But I would trust my eye, not every sound,
The ear oft catches things at false rebound.
To cleer my doubts, some told me, that did bring
By Torch-light, the dead body of the King:
When every star, like kinsmen to the dead,
That night close-mourners, hid their golden head,
And had repos'd that Royal burden, where
His people might embalm him with their tear.
Sorrow finds quick direction: I came
To a fair House, I cannot giv't a name,
It had so many, onely this I know,
It might be aptly call'd the House of wo,
Deaths Inne of late for Princes, who there lay,
As taking but a Lodging in their way
To the dark Grave. Entred the Court, I see
Many attir'd in black, but this might be
Their abstinence for Lent, for who is there
That cannot fast from Colours once a yeer?
After some justling with the guard, I came
Toth' presence, which but mockt me with a name,
For it presented nothing to my eye
But blacks, and tears for absent Majesty.
Thence to the Privie-chamber I did passe,
In hope to find him there, but there, alas!
I found new shapes of sorrow, Men whose eyes
Drunk up by tears, shew'd life in a disguise:

The mourning state here did renew my wo
For the lost Presence, Velvet hangings too
Made sorrow of more value, which beheld
The 'Scutcheon Royal in a Sable Field.
To the bed-chamber, then (the shrine some said,
Where the pale body of the King was laid)
My wild devotion brought me, This sad room
At first did fright me, opening like a Tomb,
To shew me death, where Tapers round about
Flameles, would tell me that our light was out:
But by that melancholy day was lent
I might discover on his monument
A King, with subtle Artifice so set,
My sense did stagger at the Counterfet.
Alas, was this the way to gain belief
That he was dead, to paint him now to life?
As if, when we had lost him, it had been
Enough to have thought him but alive agen:
But to these sad Remonstrances I give
No faith, the King I sought, might be alive,
For all these figures, and their Makers be
(At least as my soul wish'd) more dead then he.
From thence to hite-hall, when I came, with wing▪
Nimble as fear could make, I found the King,
I triumph'd here, and boldly did revive,
King James not dead, he was in Charles alive.

Upon the Death of Sr. Th. Nevill

Swelling Eyes forbear to weep,
Can the marble that doth keep
So rich a Nevill, not appear
Full of cold drops without your tear?
Or the Earth beneath his Tombe
Not feel a labour in her wombe,
When with her profaner dust
His ashes mingle? Sure it must
Break with burden of new pain,
And from her root he grow again.

An Elegie Upon the Honourable, Fair, and Vertuous M. Borlase

Come hither Virgins that are good, and fair,
Insteed of flowers, here carelesse strew your hair,

Pay down the tribute due from all your eyes,
For underneath this dewy Marble lies
One, worth you all; although you cannot make
Her live again, 'tis justice for her sake
To weep your selves blind, for in vain you keep
Your eye-sight, while Marya's gone to sleep,
That was your path and Leader: but away,
You are but common mourners, for this day,
Hid in a storm of tears doth wait the name
Of great Borlase, wounded, and led by fame.
The mist is blown away, I see it come
With temper'd hast to look into her Tomb
To find an arme, which from his body rent,
Does lie enbalmd in this white monument:
Forbear chief mourner, and consent to be
Without this limb, more must be torne from thee,
And kept by death, till the whole body meet,
And sleep together in one winding sheet.

Upon the Death of C. D. Engineere, Who Died Upon Service to Which Had No Command

If we those men for gallant justifie,
Who when they are commanded on, dare die:
Tell me, how glorious shall their valour stand,
That dare like Dalby, die without command?
Though order be the life of war, the sword
And bullet will not ask us for the word:
Nor did his courage know to make a pause,
When honour call'd so loud, and such a cause
As would untame a Hermit, and make room
With his own fire to meet the Martyrdome.
All that the sons of Flegm and fear can say,
Is, that he might have liv'd, and so will they,
Like earth-wormes, safe in their owne slime, and sleep
Till the last Trumpet wake'em, and then creep
Into some Blind, and wish this worthy then
Alive to hide them in some Turfes agen.
But his soul, wing'd with nobler flame, found out
Not to be active, is the way about
To Glory, which he being fond to taste,
They are too wise that blame him for his haste.

Epitaph On the Duke of Buckungham

Here lies the best and worst of Fate,
Two Kings delight, the peoples hate,
The Courtiers star, the Kingdoms eye,
A man to draw an Angel by.
Fears despiser, Villiers glory,
The Great mans volume, all times story.

An Elegie Upon the Truly Honourable Tho. Viscount Savage

Is Savage dead? and can the Rock which bears
His Name, not strait dissolve it self in tears,
And weep into the Sea? where it may have
A Burial too, whilst every frighted wave
At this new guest may raise his curled head,
And in a storm tell all the world who's dead?
But here's no want of Flood, for every eye
Conspires in melting to an Elegie.
But first, see where the King and Queen are come
To pour their grief into their servants Tombe,
Let publike sorrow be first serv'd, 'tis cleer,
The Kingdom weeps in every Princes tear,
And now his children drop their pious rain,
(Though none can soften his stiffe clay again)
And sigh, they had a Father, from whose care
And wealth in vertue, every Child's an Heir.
Their Tribute paid, close not the shrine, see where
The Treasure of his bosome doth appear.
Now coming to her Saint with her drown'd eyes,
(For sorrow leads her where her dead Lord lies)
To whose pale Relique she devoutly payes
A kisse, as holy as his life, and prayes
With many tears, till quite dissolv'd in them,
She seems contriv'd into a walking stream,
As Destiny had meant her to descend
From Rivers, but to satisfie this end.
More sorrow doth attend this herse, for here's
A train of Lords that follow, though no Peers,
For all the stock of honour is too low
for competition, yet upon this woe
Wait all that in Nobility are good,
And he that weeps not, hath no gentle blood.
Nor are these all the Mourners, see how fast
The Reer advances, I suspect their hast
And weight may overbear his Sepulcher:
Friends to the dead, contain your selves, nor fear
You that were servants, crowding to the urne

Of your dead lord, but you'l have time to mourn
This your immortal losse. But why among
Set shapes of mourning, suffer ye to throng,
Those that prophane his monument, the poor?
What make they at his tomb, and leave his door?
He was their bread, and miracles not gone,
They hope to find it in his Funeral stone:
He gave the blind men eyes too, and they can
Do no lesse now, then weep them out again.
Be sorrow free for all men, since he dies
Worth love of heaven, and the worlds sacrifice.

Upon Mr. Charles Beaumont Who Died of a Consumption

While others drop their tears upon thy herse,
Sweet Charles, and sigh to increase the wind, my verse
Pious in naming thee, cannot complain
Of death, or fate, for they were lately slain
By thy own conflict; and since good men know
What Heaven to such a Virgin Saint doth owe;
Though some will say they saw thee dead, yet I
Congratulate thy life and victory:
Thy flesh an upper garment, that it might
Aide thy eternal progresse, first grew light:
Nothing but Angel now, which thou wer't neer
Almost reduc'd to thy first Spirit here:
But fly fair soul, while our complaints are just,
That cannot follow for our chains of dust.

The Passing Bell

Hark, how chimes the Passing bell,
There's no musick to a knell;
All the other sounds we hear,
Flatter, and but cheat our ear.
This doth put us still in mind
That our flesh must be resign'd,
And a general silence made,
The world be muffled in a shade;
He that on his pillow lies
Tear enbalm'd before he dies,
Carries like a sheep his life,
To meet the sacrificers knife,
And for eternity is prest,

Sad Bell-weather to the rest.

Et longum Formosa Vale.—Friendship, Or Verses Sent to a Lover, in Answer of a Copie Which He Had Writ in Praise of his Mistris

O How I blush, to have ador'd the face
Of any Mistris, when I gave the grace,
For which I rob'd the flowers. How I did swear
Her eyes were stars, and loves soft nets her hair?
Disgrac'd the chiming of the Spheres, to tell
Her voice: and in her breath, profest to smell
The Eastern spices on the Phoenix pile:
And for her Chin, and Forehead, did beguil
Heaven of his milky way: these trimmings must
Be paid again, they're taken all on trust.
But let the Mistris thou dost serve, be fair
With her owne beauty, as some such there are
Compound with the whole sex, to make a mind
Include the Graces of fair woman-kind;
I shall not think her worth my praise, or smile,
And yet I have a Mistris all this while,
But am a convert from that Sex, and can
Reduc'd to my discretion, love a man,
With Honour, and Religion; Such a one
As dares be singly vertuous gainst the Town;
A man that's learned too, and for his parts
Is held a Prodigie of all the Arts;
A man of a cleer soul, bold, temperate, free,
Fortune and Passion wear his liverie,
And do obey; and when he will resigne
To mirth, is in at all things, but the Wine:
Of an extraction Noble, and to do
Him and the wonder right, he is young too:
As handsome as thy Mistris, more divine,
And hath no fault but that I call him mine:
My jealousie doth cloud his name, 'tis fit,
Nor art thou ripe for thy conversion yet.

The Garden

This Garden does not take my eyes,
Though here you shew how art of men
Can purchase Nature at a price
Would stock old Paradise agen.

These glories while you dote upon,
I envie not your Spring nor pride,
Nay boast the Summer all your own,
My thoughts with lesse are safisfied.
Give me a little plot of ground,
Where might I with the Sun agree,
Though every day he walk the Round,
My Garden he should seldom see.
Those Tulips that such wealth display,
To court my eye, shall lose their name,
Though now they listen, as if they
Expected I should praise their flame.
But I would see my self appear
Within the Violets drooping head,
On which a melancholy tear
The discontented Morne hath shed.
Within their budds let Roses sleep,
And virgin Lillies on their stemme,
Till sighes from Lovers glide, and creep
Into their leaves to open them.
I th' Center of my ground compose
Of Bayes and Ewe my Summer room,
Which may so oft as I repose,
Present my Arbour, and my Tombe.
No woman here shall find me out,
Or if a chance do bring one hither,
Ile be secure, for round about
Ile moat it with my eyes foul weather.
No Bird shall live within my pale,
To charme me with their shames of Art,
Unlesse some wandring Nightingale
Come here to sing, and break her heart.
Upon whose death I'le try to write
An Epitaph in some funeral stone,
So sad, and true, it may invite
My self to die, and prove mine owne.

Curse

Woman, I cannot call thee worse,
For thy vow-break, take this curse,
May that man whom thy embrace
Shall make happy in my place,
At a time when all thy blood
Lust hath poyson'd, and no good
Left in a thought, strike with that aire

He breathes upon thee next, despair,
Some death in his curld forehead fit,
And every kisse more cold then it:
Yet live, and my revenger be;
For when thou dost this Gorgon see,
Betwixt thy horror, and no doubt
But that thou art a stone throughout;
With some knife or poniard wound
Thy heart, till falling to the ground,
And pale, the world beleeve thee dead,
But not one tear upon thee shed.
No matter where thy spirit flies,
Or whose pity close thine eyes.

To the Proud M.

Proud woman, know I am above
As much thy anger as thy love:
I did once think thou hadst a face;
But when next thou tak'st thy glasse,
If thou canst see through so much paint,
Pray to thy owne; no more my Saint;
Thy eyes, those glouring twinnes, shall be
No more misleading fires to me;
Nor hope they shall continue bright,
For I will curse out all their light:
But this would shew that I were vext,
And so thy Tryimph might be next
That thou should'st force me into rage:
No, I will laugh thee into age,
Strike wrinkles on thy brow, and not
Discompose my pleasant thought,
Till thou, thy Witches face despise,
And grow angry with their eyes,
Thus wretched thou shalt wish to die,
But late obtain it; and when I
Have jeerd thee into dead and rotten,
Ile throw thee into quite forgotten.

Cupid Ungodded

Why how now Cupid, grown so wild?
So great a Tyrant, and a Child?
What wert thou but an empty shade,

Until our superstition made
Thee first a God? Blind, young, to be
A soft and harmeles Deitie.
Our Fancy gave thee that rich pair
Of Wings, to wanton in the ayre:
Thy gaudy Quiver, and thy Bow,
And golden shafts we did bestow,
But for no other exercise
Then to kill Bees, or Butterflies.
But since thou hast employ'd thy darts
Onely to wound thy Makers hearts,
And that thy wings serve but to flie
From Lovers, when they bleeding die;
Thy Blindnesse us'd but to invite
Our pitty, till we lose our sight,
Thy weaknes, not through want of yeers,
But from the Surfet of our Tears;
Stoop to the Justice of thy fate,
We can unmake that did create.
And first give back (ingrateful Thing)
To us that made thy glorious wing
Those painted feathers thou shalt find
Contemnd, and tost by every wind,
Till wandring in some night, they are
The mark of a prodigious star,
And blasted; these the world shall name
The spotted wings of evil fame:
Next, give thy arrows back, which we
Did mean for Love, not Cruelty.
That rich enamell'd bow is mine,
Come, that gay quiver too resigne,
And shining Belt; These will I burne,
And keep their ashes in some urne,
Till open'd on that solemn day,
When men to souls sad requiems pay:
Lovers shall curse, and sigh, and make
A new Letany for thy sake.
But thou art still alive; and be;
To murder, were to pitie thee.
Know wretch, thou shalt not die, before
I see thee begging at some dore:
And taken for a Vagrant stript,
Then by a furious Beadle whipt,
No more with Roses, but with Thorn:
To all the world thus made a scorn,
Ile give thee Eyes before we part,
To see thy shame, and breake thy heart.

Fye on Love

Now fye on foolish love, it not befits
Or man or woman know it.
Love was not meant for People in their wits,
And they that fondly shew it,
Betray the straw, and feathers in their braine,
And shall have Bedlem for their paine:
If single Love be such a curse,
To marry is to make it ten times worse.

To a Beautiful Lady

A way with handsome faces, let me see
Hereafter nothing but deformity;
Ill-favour'd Ladies may have souls, and those
In a capacity to be sav'd, who knows?
All that are fair are false, and if you find
A middle essence here of woman-kind,
Party par pale they are, and curst to be
Halting betwixt mishape and perjury.
Madam, put on your mask, your eyes have lost
Their charm; your beauty be at your owne cost.
I am ashore, go muster up the Train
Of Mermaids, I am deaf to every strain;
And will so voice their story to wise men,
They shall not spawn upon the Land agen.
Farewel fond love for ever! but to be
Safe in my soul, I could want charity.

Dialogue

I.
I Prethee tell me what prodigious fate
Hath discomplexion'd thee of late?

II.
Love that doth change all minds and men,
Hath thus transformed me, and when
Thou seest her heavenly face.

I.

Describe her then.

II.

Her Hairs are Cupids nets. which when she spreads,
She catches hearts and maidenheads;
Her Forehead the white Alpes doth show,
Or rather 'tis a shrine of snow,
To which with fear approaching Pilgrims bow.
Her Eye-browes are loves bowes, from which her eyes
Do never shoot, but some man dies:
Her cheeks like two fair gardens rise,
With the choise flowers of Paradise.
Her lips disclose where Musicks Temple is.
Her Tongue I call Loves Lightning, but the Throne
Of Graces is her Neck alone,
Or Poets may inspired say
There the wanton Doves do play,
When Venus means to make it Holyday.

I.

No more for shame? how hath thy fancy straid;
What a Chimera hast thou made
To dote upon? what would I give
Old Michael Angelo to revive?
Make Titian, Vandike, or bold Ruben live?
But suppose one of them, or all their Art
Should paint this darling of thy heart
A net, a rock, a shrine of snow,
A Church, a garden, and a bow,
Is't not a pretty face compounded so?
Or if a Pencil, and their hand should make
A flame of Lightning, who will take
This for a tongue? Or if men see
A Throne, Doves billing two or three,
Who will commend this for a neck but thee?
Collect thy scatter'd sence (poor man) be wise,
Love, but first give thy reason eyes;
Thy fancie bears all like a flood;
Reduce them to their flesh and blood,
And Women then are hardly understood.

A Postscript to the Reader

I had no intention upon the birth of these Poems, to let them proceed to the Publik view, forbearing in my owne modesty to interpose my Fancies, when I see the World so plentifully furnished. But when I observed most of these Copies corrupted in their transcripts, and the rest fleeting from me, which were by some indiscreet Collector not acquainted with distributive Justice, mingled with other mens (some Eminent) conceptions in Print, I thought my self concern'd to use some vindication, and reduce them to my owne, without any pride or designe of deriving opinion from their worth, but to shew my charity, that other innocent men should not answer for my vanities.

If thou best Curteous, Reader, there are some errors of the Presse scattered, which thy Clemency will not lay to my charge: Other things I remit to thy judgement: If thou beest modest, I repent not to have exposed them and my self to thy censure.

James Shirley

JAMES SHIRLEY – A CONCISE BIBLIOGRAPHY

The following includes years of first publication, and of performance if known, together with dates of licensing by the Master of the Revels if available.

TRAGEDIES
The Maid's Revenge (licensed 9th February 1626; printed, 1639)
The Traitor (licensed 4th May 1631; printed, 1635)
Love's Cruelty (licensed 14th November 1631; printed, 1640)
The Politician (acted, 1639; printed, 1655)
The Cardinal (licensed 25th May 1641; printed, 1652).

TRAGI-COMEDIES
The Grateful Servant (licensed 3rd November 1629 as The Faithful Servant; printed 1630)
The Young Admiral (licensed 3rd July 1633; printed 1637)
The Coronation (licensed 6th February 1635, as Shirley's, but printed in 1640 as a work of John Fletcher)
The Duke's Mistress (licensed 18th January 1636; printed 1638)
The Gentleman of Venice (licensed 30th October 1639; printed 1655)
The Doubtful Heir (printed 1652), licensed as Rosania, or Love's Victory in 1640
The Imposture (licensed 10th November 1640; printed 1652)
The Court Secret (printed 1653).

COMEDIES
Love Tricks, or the School of Complement (licensed 10th February 1625; printed under its subtitle, 1631)
The Wedding (ca. 1626; printed 1629)
The Brothers (licensed 4th November 1626; printed 1652)
The Witty Fair One (licensed 3rd October 1628; printed 1633)
The Humorous Courtier (licensed 17th May 1631; printed 1640).
The Changes, or Love in a Maze (licensed 10th January 1632; printed 1639)
Hyde Park (licensed 20th April 1632; printed 1637)
The Ball (licensed 16th November 1632; printed 1639)
The Bird in a Cage, or The Beauties (licensed 21st January 1633; printed 1633)
The Gamester (licensed 11th November 1633; printed 1637)
The Example (licensed 24th June 1634; printed 1637)
The Opportunity (licensed 29th November 1634; printed 1640)

The Lady of Pleasure (licensed 15th October 1635; printed 1637)
The Royal Master (acted and printed 1638)
The Constant Maid, or Love Will Find Out the Way (printed 1640)
The Sisters (licensed 26th April 1642; printed 1653).
Honoria and Mammon (printed 1659)

DRAMAS
A Contention for Honor and Riches (printed 1633), morality play
The Triumph of Peace (licensed 3rd February 1634; printed 1634), masque
The Arcadia (printed 1640), pastoral tragicomedy
St. Patrick for Ireland (printed 1640), neo-miracle play
The Triumph of Beauty (ca. 1640; printed 1646), masque
The Contention of Ajax and Ulysses (printed 1659), entertainment
Cupid and Death (performed 26th March 1653; printed 1659), masque

www.ingramcontent.com/pod-product-compliance
Lightning Source LLC
Chambersburg PA
CBHW070111070426
42448CB00038B/2509